THE CHURCH MUSICIANS GUILD OF BUFFALO:

FROM CATHOLIC CHOIRMASTERS TO CHURCH MUSICIANS 1946–2021

Bill Fay
Past Director
Church Musicians Guild of Buffalo

NFB Publishing
Buffalo, New York

NFB
NFB Publishing/Amelia Press
119 Dorchester Road
Buffalo, New York 14213

For more information visit Nfbpublishing.com

Dedicated to the Cooney Sisters, all graduates of Nazareth College
Catherine Cooney Wilhelm, my aunt and godmother
Alice Cooney, my aunt and Sister of Saint Joseph
Mary Cooney Fay, my mother and liturgical musician

Table of Contents

PREFACE

T HE CHURCH MUSICIANS Guild of Buffalo has an illustrious history dating back to 1946. The 19th century reform of Catholic Church music influenced the Leo Roy family who so strongly led the development of liturgical music in the diocese of Buffalo. This legacy has served as the foundation of the Guild when it became a chapter of the National Association of Pastoral Musicians in 1983.

The Church Musicians Guild is unique in that we are made up of professional and avocational musicians, liturgists, clergy and just plain folks who love liturgical music. We are a lively bunch who love God, our church, and its musical heritage.

It was my privilege to lead the chapter for six years and to document its history. This heritage needs to be passed on to the next generation of church musicians so that they may in turn teach those coming up about the efforts that have been made to make musical liturgy normative in our diocese.

In the fall of 2021, the Church Musicians Guild observes its 75th anniversary.

The Guild is the oldest chapter of the National Association of Pastoral Musicians in existence today. To our pioneers who laid the foundation, we give thanks. To the young people just beginning work in liturgical music, we offer you inspiration. For the reader, I hope you will come to respect the history of the Guild, its European antecedents, and its American development from the Midwest to Buffalo, New York.

Bill Fay
September 1, 2019
Kenmore, New York

THE CECILIAN MOVEMENT AND JOHN SINGENBERGER

THE ORIGINS OF the Church Musicians Guild are rooted in our heritage of liturgical music from the nineteenth century. In the 1860's, there was a movement in Germany to purge Catholic Church services from the influence of operatic elements in worship. This movement resulted in the creation of a philosophy to promote an outlook that sought the restoration of Gregorian chant and renaissance polyphony to church services. This movement, called Cecilianism, resulted in a likeminded group of musicians who formed the Society of Saint Cecelia. The movement originated in the city of Regensburg, formerly Ratisbon, Germany. Austria and Switzerland were influenced by this thought. The first musician to be considered is John Singenberger who became a follower of the Cecilian movement during his study in Regensburg.

John Singenberger was born in 1848 in Kirchberg, Switzerland, and received his training in organ and choral work at school under the influence of Father Franz Witt in Regensburg. He developed a friendship with the officers of the Pustet Publishing Company, which printed his first book. Singenberger and Max Spiegler were invited to come to the New World in 1873 by Father Joseph Salzman, the founder and rector of Saint Francis de Sales Seminary of the Diocese of Milwaukee, who was looking for just the right men to begin teaching in the newly founded Catholic Normal School at Saint Francis, Wisconsin, near Milwaukee. Opening in 1871, this school would graduate almost 500 men who would serve churches in the Midwest as school teachers and church organists. Later, the Pio Nono College was founded to offer commercial subjects suited for business employment. These two institutions were later merged. It is estimated that Singenberger taught almost one thousand students at the school, although many did not graduate. There were only 70-80 students at any one time.

Singenberger was an indefatigable worker for the cause of correct liturgical music. His career was spent in three areas: the instruction of young men to be teacher-organists, the teaching of Sisters in summer schools throughout the Midwest, and the activities of the American version of the Society of Saint Cecelia through conventions and publications. As a teacher at the Catholic Normal School, the maestro was engaged in instruction for many hours per day. Only German was spoken in the school, and Singenberger exhibited a focus and discipline characteristic of German culture. He taught organ, violin, choir, chant, harmony, conducting, piano and liturgy.

After assistant professor Spielger returned to Europe in 1876, Singenberger gave all the music instruction for about 24 years. His work schedule would cost him his marriage and his health.

By 1920, when the golden jubilee of the school was celebrated, the Catholic Normal School was also offering a four year course in church music based on the *Motu Proprio* of Pope Pius X. Graduates in music specifically were listed in the jubilee book beginning in 1907.

Singenberger's home was across the street from the school, and this is where he and his wife Carolina raised their children. It was said that his temperament was much softer with his family. The maestro and his wife had six children during their marriage: Johanna, Joseph, Dorothea, Myra, Otto, and Carlo; two children would be important to this study.

Otto followed his father in the music profession after graduation from

Catholic Normal in 1898. A daughter, Myra, married Caspar Koch, who graduated from the school in 1892. Koch later moved to Pittsburgh where his son, Paul, developed the well-known program at Saint Paul's Cathedral with its Von Beckerath pipe organ. Caspar Koch is one of the signatories in the 1890 yearbook from Catholic Normal in the possession of Leo Roy's granddaughter, Eileen Roy.

Otto went to Munich to study music and returned to the United States. He took over for his father when he was later hospitalized, served as music director of Mundelein Seminary, and supervised music education in the schools of the diocese of Milwaukee. At one time, he served as organist at Saint Louis Church, Buffalo, for one year. Otto passed away in 1944.

In the golden jubilee booklet for the Catholic Normal School, there is a listing of a student from Swormville, New York, named Aloysius Beiter who graduated in 1896. One would assume that Beiter knew Roy from Saint Mary's Church and perhaps went to Saint Francis upon Roy's recommendation.

During the summers, Singenberger traveled to various cities to give instruction to the Sisters. Many complained about his strict markings of their harmony assignments and demanding corrections in choir. His favorite Sisters were the School Sisters of Saint Francis, who began in Campbellsport, Wisconsin, and later settled in Milwaukee. He taught the well-known Sister Cherubim whose father founded the Schaefer Organ Company. Sister began the Saint Joseph Conservatory and published many compositions for church and school use. The momentum in this community resulted in the merger of the conservatory with Alverno College. This school was renowned for its programs in music education, liturgical music, and music therapy. The most prominent Sister from this community was Sister Theophane Hytrek, PhD, who performed in Buffalo in 1982 at the invitation of the guild. Hytrek was a Fellow of the American Guild of Organists and received a doctorate in composition from the Eastman School of Music in 1957. So it could be said that Sister Theophane's teachers were formed in the tradition of the Cecilian movement through the tutelage of Singenberger, and that she carried the tradition forward. Jim Kosnik said that, in conversations with him, Sister Theophane frequently referred to Singenberger's role in her community's music development.

As president of the Society of Saint Cecelia, Singenberger served as the leader of the Cecilian movement in the United States. He was also editor of a German language newsletter called *The Cecelia* and, briefly, an English language newspaper. This movement was able to influence many outside the immediate area of the Midwest. The maestro said that the goals of the Society were to restore simplicity to the music of the church services, to promote Gregorian chant, to encourage congregational singing in the vernacular as allowed by authorities, and to offer systematic instruction in chant in the parochial schools.

During the summers, Singenberger would lead conventions in major cities to promote Cecilian music. Rochester, New York, was the site of two conventions. This ceased in 1904 after the promulgation of Pope Pius X's document on church music, *Tra Le Solleciitudini* (*On the Restoration of Sacred Music*) which forbade the use of women in the church choir. The 1904 convention was cancelled, and this obedient musician was not able to initiate further choral conventions in this country. After 1904, subscriptions to the magazine *Cecelia* dropped. Singenberger commented: "When the Church speaks, then we have nothing to say."

The Cecilian movement did achieve many of its goals: it eliminated the operatic aspects of the Viennese school and musical instruments other than the organ. Requiem mass settings replaced hymns at funerals, children were trained to sing the ordinary of the mass in chant, solo singing was minimized, and boy choirs replaced women in the church choir. Palestrina was considered the composer of choice, and many Cecilian masses were written in imitation of this Renaissance master.

Another result of the *Motu Propio* was the publication of the Vatican-mandated Solemnes version of chant over the previous Ratisbon edition in 1905. The difference in interpretation focused on the rhythm of chant. This difference of opinion would surface later in Buffalo in the 1950's.

The composer wrote 17 masses, 6 vesper services, 20 Benediction hymns, 16 motets, and five instruction books. Yet Singenberger experienced many sorrows in his life. His son Joseph died unexpectedly, and his daughter Dorothea died during childbirth. His wife became estranged from him due to his many absences from home and left him in 1904. According to the testimony of daughter-in-law, Mrs. Otto Singenberger, Carolina requested a legal separation and a sum of $2000. She left Wisconsin with another man and moved to Portland, Oregon. Using the name Madame Lenieux, she established an artist colony where she taught painting. Singenberger never saw his wife again. This scandal affected the maestro deeply, resulting in his admission to a sanatorium for three years of therapy from 1904 to 1907. His son, Otto, took over in the professor's absence.

Singenberger eventually recovered his health and resumed his heavy schedule of teaching, composing, and writing editorials. Otto stayed on until 1910. To relieve the heavy work load, Singenberger enjoyed the assistance of Father Frindolin Walter, a Swiss native who studied music in Paris with Guilmant, Vierne, and Breitbach.

Throughout many years of service, Singenberger was formally recognized several times. He received papal honors from Pope Leo XIII as a knight of the Society of Saint Gregory in 1882. An honorary doctorate (LLD) was given him by the University of Notre Dame in 1895. He received the papal cross in 1905. The highest honor given to a layman was bestowed on the maestro in 1908 with the designation "Commander of the Order of Saint Sylvester." He died in 1924 and is buried in a small cemetery near his home and school in Saint Francis, Wisconsin. The well-known Father Carlo Rossini said that Singenberger was the greatest Catholic Church musician in America. Singenberger was consulted by the trustees of Saint Louis Church for the installation of the Kimball pipe organ in 1902.

One of the many students that Singenberger taught and who was to influence a generation of musicians in Buffalo was Leo Roy.

LEO ROY AND HIS FAMILY

THE CATHOLIC NORMAL School trained a generation of German teacher-organists who influenced the music of Catholic worship primarily in the Midwest. However, one graduate came to western New York to work for Saint Mary's Church in Swormville (East Amherst). His name was Leo Roy, and he would have a major influence on the music of our diocese.

Mr. Roy's family emigrated from the Alsace-Lorraine area of Europe through Quebec, Canada, and settled in Prairie du Rocher in Illinois. This community no longer exists. Roy was born in 1870 or 1871 and spoke French and German. He matriculated in the Catholic Normal School and graduated in 1890. Roy came to our area and worked for Saint Mary's Church in Swormville for a few years. It was at this time that he met Magdelena Heckman, and they were married at Saint Ann's Church in Buffalo. Roy served as teacher, organist, and sexton at Saint Mary's Church and left this parish possibly as a result of the heavy workload. Roy then worked in Indiana, and, later in 1908, he accepted a position as music director for Saint Mary's of the Assumption Church in Lancaster, where he would remain for 46 years.

Roy's granddaughter, Eileen Roy (daughter of Imelda), remembers him as quiet and reserved with a dry sense of humor. It was rare for her grandfather not to be dressed in coat and tie. In fact, when working in the garden, Roy would put on coveralls over his dress clothes. Her grandmother was more feisty. Mrs. Roy is remembered for her outstanding work as a seamstress. A christening gown that she embroidered is still in the possession of the family.

Carmel Besch Metzger remembers Roy in the late 1940's. She attended the parochial high school and sang in the glee club, for which Roy served as the accompanist. She noted that he was always properly dressed in coat and tie and was a distinguished gentleman. Several of Carmel's friends remember him as "always there," which would make sense since the parish provided a house for the Roy family next door to the church.

The choir of Saint Mary's was known for the quality of its performance, and Roy is also remembered for his studio teaching of piano and violin. Roy played a Felgemaker pipe organ which is still in use today. He died in 1955 and is buried in the parish cemetery. His wife passed away three years later. What is remarkable about Roy was that he encouraged his ten children to be musicians. His wife, Magdalen, served as organist of Saint James Church in Depew for 33 years. Four daughters, Cecelia, Collette, Gertrude, and Marnie, served as organists in our area.

Collette McFarland was trained as a nurse. However, she played organ at Saint John the Baptist Church, Buffalo for 24 years. Mrs. McFarland spent the subsequent 18 years at Saint Aloysius Gonzaga Church in Cheektowaga. She commented on the poor compensation the organists received: "The idea was to just have someone there to play but to give them as little as possible. And did we work!"

Gertrude Maitland played the organ at Holy Angels Church while studying at D'Youville College. She served as music director for many years at Trinity Episcopal Church in Lancaster. Mrs. Maitland studied the organ with DeWitt Garretson and Helen Townsend as well as Han Vigeland.

The fourth daughter was Margaret (Marnie) Rozler. She played organ at Our Lady of Pompeii Church, Lancaster about 1935. Later she moved into the family homestead next to St. Mary's Church where she played the organ and directed the choir at Saint Mary's for 37 years, retiring in 1987. Her husband served as mayor of the village of Lancaster. She passed away in 2010.

Eileen Roy recalls that it was said that Marie's playing was like her father's, not like her Aunt Cecilia's performance. Joe Rozler commented that his mother had a lyrical sense, performing with a beautiful voice and soft registrations on the organ. She did not consider herself an organist, just a "hymn player."

Marnie's son, Joseph, was the only grandchild of Leo Roy to study music professionally. He grew up in the house next to the church where he played in the parish cemetery and learned to sleep with church bells ringing at all hours and trains passing in the night. Joe did not know his grandparents well but knew his mother's sisters well. He loved to visit his Aunt Imelda. Since Cecelia Kenny did not have children, Joseph saw her as more aloof. He remembers that his Aunt Cecelia wrote a theory workbook that was published. Joe also maintains that his grandfather taught band in the Saint Mary's parochial school. Mrs. Kenny was a mentor to Joe, often giving him gifts of classical recordings that he did not appreciate until he was older. Joe was fortunate to inherit Mrs. Kenny's grand piano.

The daughters have described their family life in the home as forming a little orchestra on Sunday afternoons. Marie Rozler has said of that time: "Mother would play the piano or cello. Gert was the first violin. Dad played second violin. Imelda would play the viola and Cecelia the cello. Thomas and Marie played the bass and Norb the trombone. Collette played the piano, and I played the cello. It was a lot of fun." According to Eileen Roy, boyfriends would come to call at the house on Sunday and would have to wait till the orchestral hour was over to visit with their young ladies.

There were two pianos in the living room, so playing four hand duets was common practice. The sisters described Cecelia Kenny as the one who had been most active in promoting the continuing education and support of church organists. She is so important to the history of the Guild that she warrants her own chapter.

CECELIA ROY KENNY

Cecelia Marie Roy Kenny is arguably the most renowned liturgical musician of the 20th century in the Diocese of Buffalo. She wore many hats and is listed in the Buffalo directory of fine arts in the 1920's as a teacher of piano. Cecelia was born in Buffalo on September 25, 1898, the eldest child of Leo and Magdelena Roy and listed as living intermittently since birth as a resident of Buffalo. She completed high school at Stella Niagara Seminary in 1914. In the 1920's, Cecelia lived on Leroy Avenue and played the organ at Blessed Trinity Church. In addition, she performed for the Chromatic Club, American Artists Club, the Buffalo Athletic Club, and at Sacred Heart Academy. Her performances were broadcast on the radio.

Many are unaware of the diversity of Cecelia's talents. Although she is remembered as a daughter of a distinguished musical family, Cecelia claimed that her first love was flying airplanes, well documented by an essay she wrote and deposited in the Buffalo History Museum. When Cecelia married Thomas Kenny in 1928, she was introduced to a world of aviation that grew after the successful Lindbergh's trans-Atlantic flight. Her husband, a native of England, came to Buffalo in the mid 1920's to serve as Secretary and Treasurer of Consolidated Aircraft Corporation. A flying school was established, and Tom, Cecelia, and her brother Norbert began flight instruction in 1929. Cecelia was the first "girl" to solo at the Buffalo Airport and the first "girl" to be licensed in Buffalo. Her brother subsequently became air traffic controller #1 at La Guardia Airport in New York City. Cecelia and her husband purchased an 80-acre farm on Transit Road to build a hangar and a home for the Kenny family. However, Kenny Flying Service also operated out of the Buffalo Airport, so the home was never built. Many of the flying related activities were routine, such as aircraft sales and service, charter flights, sight-seeing trips, penny-a-pound (per person) flights for ten minutes on Sunday, serial advertising, serial photography, and parachute testing.

Cecelia remembered that "I never thought one way or the other about it being unusual for a woman; then one day I made my first solo, someone came over and told me they'd looked into it and found I was the first woman to solo here. The next day there was a whole battery of photographers around." Cecelia remembers helping stranded fishermen on an ice floe in Lake Erie by dropping food and supplies until they could be rescued. Her training included aerobatics such as stalls, spins, wing-overs, loops, rolls, and falling leaf and Immelmann turns. Despite Cecelia's experience in flying, she did have one near accident when one of the engine's cylinders cracked resulting in flames shooting out of the side of the engine. Fortunately, she was able to land safely without injury. This pilot also flew people over Niagara Falls and to Florida.

Her picture appeared in the Buffalo Evening News in 1967 detailing her former aviation career. The picture, taken in 1932, features a handsome woman wearing a leather jacket, helmet, and goggles in an open cockpit. When told that Cecelia was not the type to be a pilot, she responded that "the women in aviation were always a refined group."

In the course of the depression, the Kenny Flying Service experienced turmoil, and several planes were lost through student pilot error. The restriction of credit put the company in a financial bind. These setbacks were a great strain on Thomas Kenny, resulting in a massive heart attack, and he died soon after in 1935. He was 42 years old, and the couple had been married for only six years. Family members said that Cecelia adored her husband and was devastated when he passed away. She wrote that his death: "...spelled 'finis' to my career in the management side of the aviation industry. Flying had become my first love, and I wanted desperately to be able to earn a livelihood as an aircraft pilot. However, the airlines would not consider employing a woman in that capacity. I notice that times haven't changed! My only alternative was then to go back to my former profession--music. I was engaged as organist at Immaculate Conception Church in Buffalo, and I also got a job doing secretarial work and accounting at Meadowbrook Country Club. When I transferred to Saint Joseph's Old Cathedral as organist in 1938, the schedule became so demanding that I had to give up the work at Meadowbrook." She continued: "In retrospect, I would say that the flying years were by far the most interesting, fascinating and exciting period of my life. We met so many pioneering "greats" (trail blazers, if you will) in the aviation field and numbered among our friends the first round-the-world flyers, particularly Captain Lowell Smith, Eric Nelson, and Leigh Wade, the Flying Hutchinsons, etc." Cecelia is listed as one of The Ninety-Nines Pioneer Women Aviators who are honored on the website and in The Ninety-Nines Museum of Women Pilots Building dedicated to the history of women pilots and located at the airport of Oklahoma City.

The rest of this chapter is devoted to Cecelia's career in liturgical music. Her influence in liturgical music began with leadership in the Church Musicians Guild after World War II. Many of the church organists needed help with Gregorian chant, and the Guild provided the education needed for this training. Cecelia served the Guild as corresponding secretary and president for two terms.

Cecelia pursued continuing education before that became commonplace, having studied church music at Pius X School of Liturgical Music in New York City and at Saint John's University in Minnesota. Her work culminated in a Bachelor of Music degree from the University of Montreal. She acquired choral training gained at workshops given by the greats of that time, Fred Waring and Olaf and Paul Christensen.

As her workload increased in music, Cecelia taught at Rosary Hill and D'Youville Colleges and the Nardin Academy. She lectured at Community Music School and served as one of the directors of the annual diocesan children's concerts. She served at Saint Joseph Old Cathedral for forty years. This writer remembers attending an event at the cathedral to commemorate the 40th anniversary of Cecelia serving as organist. However, Robert Winkler remembers that Msgr. Loftus offered Cecelia a position with a lot more money. She left the cathedral to work at Saint Mark's Church in the fall of 1960, returning to the cathedral a year later.

Cecelia's greatest contribution was her involvement in the publication of *Cantate Omnes Hymnal.* Although conceived of as a diocesan hymnal, the book received national attention and Cecelia later opened a store to sell the hymnal and related church music publications. In 1959, Cecelia Kenny was named the recipient of the Catholic Choirmaster Liturgical Music Award, given by the Society of Saint Gregory, joining a distinguished collection of musicians including Nicola Montani, Justine Ward, Achille Bragers, Becket Gibbs, Joseph Murphy, Dom Gregory Huegle and John Fehring. The presentation was made by Bishop Joseph Burke at a ceremony held at the Hotel Statler Hilton.

Cecelia bridged the change from the Latin to English liturgy gracefully. She is remembered for her contribution towards a new Schlicker organ console for Old Saint Joseph's Cathedral.

Alexander Peloquin dedicated his Easter psalm, "This Is the Day," to Cecelia in his 1971 Songs of Israel. Some of the prominent musicians in the diocese who studied the organ with Cecelia included Ethel Graben-stetter, Father Jack Ledwon, Monsignor Paul Litwin, and Father Louis Do-linic. Dominic wrote in his memoirs that he was introduced to Cecelia by Msgr. Kawalec. Father Louis observed that "she was a wonderful person and a tough teacher--no easy way around her." Dolinic accompanied Cecelia Kenny, Henry Kawalec, Paul Eberz, Sister Ryan, Ernestine Otis, and Ethel Grabenstetter to Liturgical Weeks in Pittsburgh, Washington, and Philadelphia.

Cecelia passed away in 1980 at the age of 81. She suffered from cancer, but actually died of a heart attack. This writer attended her funeral that summer. Cecelia is remembered by her niece Eileen as very determined and with firm ideas. She remembers that men were very attracted to Cecelia's personality. Robert Chambers said that Cecelia had "her own way." Regina Dougherty remembers Cecelia as fearless yet liked to have a good time. Her drink of choice was the Rob Roy. This fact was substantiated by Eileen as well. Nephew Joe Rozler did not study music under Cecelia's direction, but for those family members who did so, they knew that she was strict, emphasizing doing things the "right way." Joe remembers his aunt as pointing out that he did not remain "within the lines" of his coloring book! David Nease remembers Cecelia as having a large studio of private students.

SISTER MARY GRACE RYAN

Sister Mary Grace Ryan provided the impetus for the creation of the Church Musicians Guild. Born in Lowell, Massachusetts in 1897 and christened Winifred Ryan, her parents were Martin, formerly of England, and Margaret McHugh, originally from Scotland. Mary Grace entered the Sisters of Saint Mary of Namur in Lockport, New York in 1913 and professed her final vows in 1922. Most of her assignments were at Saint Mary's Seminary in Buffalo and Mount Saint Mary's High School in Kenmore. At one time, she served as supervisor of music for diocesan schools.

Sister Mary Grace earned her NYS teaching certificate from Albany in 1923 and her BA from Catholic University of America in 1935. Her master's in music was earned in 1941 from the same institution with her thesis: "The Progress of Liturgical Music Since 1903." It was at this time that Sister musicians completed their coursework within Sisters College, since women were not allowed to study at the university proper during the academic year. Noteworthy instructors were Sister Agnesine, a proponent of the Ward method for teaching Gregorian chant and Dr. Conrad Bernier who taught organ and composition.

Sister Ryan founded the Buffalo chapter of the National Catholic Music Educators Association during World War II. It was in promoting that work that she addressed a need for a separate organization for church musicians; hence the Catholic Choirmaster Guild, and in 1955 she began a student chapter. Twenty students from high schools and colleges met for monthly meetings during which Sister Ryan taught organ, chant, and conducting. Students were encouraged to lend their skills and talents to their local parishes. After the first year, Father Christian Puehn came on board as moderator. Many remember Sister Ryan's work in developing student organists including Glenn Hufnagel and Robert Winkler. The later still has in his possession a Junior Organist Guild membership card from 1963.

Another aspect of Sister's leadership were concerts given by the Sisters Choir of Buffalo, sponsored by NCMEA. On April 1, 1962, the Sisters presented a program directed by Msgr. Henry Kawalec and Gerard Reinagel at Mount Saint Mary's High School, with Kawalec conducting the sacred music and Reinagel directing the secular songs. The concert included a string ensemble performed with piano accompaniment by Sister Grace. Almost one hundred women religious participated in this event.

Sister Mary Grace had a creative bent and wrote many musical compositions, some of which have been published. She also wrote poetry. In her later years, while staying at the infirmary at age 93, she was able to play an hour's worth of her compositions for visitors from the Guild. She also played the card game, gin rummy, because as she said: "it's enjoyable and stimulates the mind."

Shortly before her death, Sister Mary Grace offered her best wishes to the Guild on its 50th anniversary: "Congratulations to the Choirmasters/Church Musicians Guild on your golden anniversary. I have watched your progress and am very proud of all of you who have kept the Guild so alive. My prayers and blessings are with you."

After a long career, Sister retired to Marycrest Infirmary where she died on September 25, 1995, at the age of 97. Her funeral took place at Saint

Andrew Church, Kenmore, where she had last taught. Sister is buried in Mount Olivet Cemetery. Printed in the program for her funeral is the following text composed by Sister Ryan for her own anniversary.

Love Sings Life's Song

My life is bound with Yours, Sweet Heart, wholly forever!

All Labor now is joy, dear heart working together;

We'll gather all the flowing years in one sweet Song--

Their rhythmic waves of smiles and tears like tidal throng!

Through major or through minor key--what'er its measure--

Its melody but Love shall be--our heart's full treasure!

Past warring worlds, hand in hand,

We'll climb the stairs to peace above.

The bars of Death are only a breath in our eternal Song of Love!

Catholic Normal School, Saint Francis, Wisconsin, 1890
Leo Roy, row one, second from the right John Singenberger, second row,
fourth from the right.

Leo and Magdelena Roy wedding, 1896

Cecilia Roy Kenny

Cecilia Roy Kenny in pilot uniform

Guild choral festival 1947
Msgr. Kawalec and Robert Chambers on the right.

Cecilia Roy Kenny receiving award from Society of Saint Gregory in 1959
Msgr. Kawalec on the right. Bishop Joseph Burke on the left

Rev. Paul Eberz celebrating 25th anniversary of ordination

Sister Mary Grace Ryan teaching music lesson

Rev. Paul Eberz, Sister Mary Grace Ryan, Msgr. Henry Kawalec

Rev. Virgil Funk, founder and president of NPM 50th anniversary of guild, 1996
right of Funk is David Nease, Sr. Judith Kubicki and Mickey Dick

Rev. Louis Dolinic, Alan Lukas, Sr. Judith Kubicki, Rev. Jack Ledwon, Jeff Nowak

NPM Organ School at SUNY Fredonia
Regina Doherty on 2nd step, first on the left
Dr. Jim Kosnik, back row on the left

Frank Scinta, organist and choral director

Robert Kiercz, organist and long time guild officer

Children's Choir Festival at the former St Francis Xavier Church, 2012
Bill Fay, conductor, Melissa Herr, accompanist

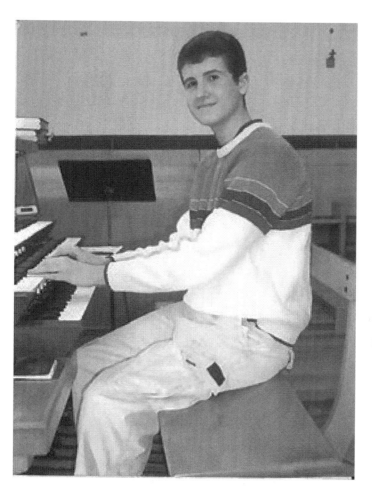

Peter Gonciarz, organ scholarship winner, 2010

MONSIGNOR HENRY KAWALEC

Arguably the most important person who dominated the music scene in the Catholic Church of Buffalo during the second half of the twentieth century was Monsignor Henry Kawalec. Many musicians and priests consulted him on liturgical music matters. His death in 1991 left a void that has never been filled. One long-time member described Kawalec's presence and visibility as much appreciated by Guild members. For instance, David Nease said that Monsignor never missed a board meeting or a Guild event.

Kawalec was born in 1916 to John and Angeline Kawalec and baptized in Saint Casimir's Church. Early evidence of a calling to a vocation to the priesthood could be seen by Henry setting up a small altar in the attic with homemade vestments and altar furnishings. This activity led the young man to enroll in the Little Seminary, Buffalo, where he mastered several languages. After that training, Henry attended Our Lady of the Angels Seminary at Niagara University, where the seminarian demonstrated musical talent by winning one dollar for singing *Pange Lingua* in solfege. The seminary leaders gave Kawalec the student choir to direct and sent him to Manhattanville College of the Sacred Heart to study chant at the well-known Pius X School of Liturgical Music. He studied there for the summers of 1941 and 1942 and probably would have come in contact with the well-known Mother Georgia Stevens who founded the school with Justine Ward. In 1941 the music school celebrated its silver anniversary with Cardinal Spellman participating. Kawalec was ordained in 1941 at Saint Joseph's New Cathedral.

For one year the young priest worked in the missionary apostolate in Cassadaga and then was assigned to Blessed Trinity Church under the pastorate of Monsignor Rung. By 1943, Father Kawalec was directing the parish choir with Ethel Grabenstatter as accompanist and was given a teaching assignment at the Little Seminary in 1944, but keeping the choir directorship.

After World War II, Kawalec was involved in the formation of the local unit of the National Catholic Music Educators Association where he worked with Sister Mary Grace. The first meeting of the Guild was held at Mount Saint Mary Academy in October 1945. Father Kawalec was elected temporary chairman with Cecelia Roy Kenny nominated as secretary.

Concurrently, Kawalec taught Greek, English, religion, and music at the Little Seminary and established a glee club of some 32 singers. One of the first tenors was Father Christian Puehn who later went on to study at the Pontifical Institute of Sacred Music and led the choir at Saint John Vianney Seminary for a number of years. Ever the life-long learner, Kawalec studied voice with Julia Mahoney to help in his work. He also worked closely with Mount Saint Joseph Academy and College where he taught workshops and chant masses with the cooperation of Sister Agnes and Sister Laura.

None of these efforts compared with the enormity of the *Cantate Omnes Hymnal* project.

Beginning in 1949, Kawalec joined Msg. Paul Eberz and Cecelia Kenny in compiling the hymn book. The tedious work commenced at Rosary Hill College. So that the hymnal could be printed at a reasonable cost, plates had to be prepared by hand and the notes lettered by hand. The well-known Sister Jeanne, head of the art department, assisted in this project.

Kawalec had additional duties at the seminary, such as prefect and vice rector. He acquired a reputation as a maintenance man. All this activity came to the notice of Bishop Burke of Buffalo who elevated Father Kawalec to the rank of monsignor in 1959. Later, when the rector of the seminary was promoted to pastor of a parish, Kawalec became the rector from 1966 to 1968. In 1966, Monsignor celebrated his 25th jubilee of ordination with a festivity given by the Guild.

In later years, Kawalec became pastor of Queen of Peace Church and, in 1974, pastor of Assumption Church, both parishes known for their large concentration of Polish families. About 1977, Msgr. Kawalec gave up his position as moderator of the Guild to Father Louis Dominic. The founder commented on his years of service to our Guild: "Being the spiritual moderator of this Guild was never a difficult task because whatever anyone might say or think about musicians, one thing is true, they are remarkable people, and doubly so when they use their talents for the glory of the Lord."

Monsignor died on June 18, 1991, after a two-week illness. Only hours before his golden jubilee celebration, the monsignor became ill. At his request, the mass and dinner went on without him. In the obituary in the Buffalo News, Kawalec was praised for his involvement of the laity in parish activities and for liturgies that reflected a post-Vatican II outlook. His sister Rita Protas survived him. He is buried at Saint Stanislaus Cemetery in Cheektowaga. David Nease remembers: "Monsignor Kawalec was always very dignified and led by example as well as word. He had great vision and shared his many talents generously." Nease felt that Kawalec was a visionary who spoke of the liturgy in the vernacular long before that was a commonly accepted ideal.

MONSIGNOR PAUL EBERZ

Father Paul Eberz is known for serving as director of the diocesan priests' choir for twenty five years. Largely self-taught, he was considered by a long-time Guild member to be a very capable musician. He also made a contribution to the publishing of the *Cantate Omnes Hymnal*.

Paul Ebeerz was born in 1907 and attended Saint Francis Xavier School. He studied at Canisius High School and College and attended the seminary at Christ the King Seminary at Saint Bonaventure University. He was ordained in 1937 and sang his first mass at Saint Francis Xavier Church. Father Eberz obtained his musical training at the seminary. He played the organ and directed the priests' choir which sang at all the priests' funerals and at three ordination/ installations of bishops. David Nease suggested that this innovation was created at the time when concelebration was not the norm in the church, therefore allowing the visiting priests to sing in the choir.

Father Eberz was appointed papal chamberlain with the title of monsignor in 1959. He attended the Liturgical Conference in 1944 and left that event with the idea that people should not be silent when they gathered together in worship. That may have led to his commitment to developing the diocesan hymnbook. He also helped to plan the music for the 1947 Eucharistic Congress which brought nearly 100,000 persons to Delaware Park in Buffalo. Speaking of congregational singing, Eberz said that "people are always comfortable with what they know. To learn new things for a 60-70 year old person is difficult. Participation at our ten o'clock mass is really great. Good musicians help." His support of the music program led to the renovation of the 1911 pipe organ at Saint Mary's Church, Lockport, which was his last assignment. Other assignments included St Stephen, Grand Island, St. Martin, Langford, Holy Cross, St. Francis Xavier, St. Joachim, and St. Joseph, the remaining parishes located in Buffalo. Ebert also served as chaplain at St. Mary's Hospital in Niagara Falls.

Ebert was most well-known for advocating for civil rights while pastor of Saint Nicholas and Sacred Heart Churches on the east side of Buffalo, and in 1964 he marched on the nation's capital for civil rights. Ecumenism was another interest of his, and in 1980 he received a Brotherhood Award from the Lockport chapter of the National Conference of Christians and Jews. Canisius College honored him with a Doctorate of Humane Letters in 1967. Msgr. Eberz was also a member of the priests' senate.

In the Guild newsletter, Father Paul Bossi remembered his colleague with comments that he heard from Holy Cross parishioners: "He was the singing priest" and "He always had the kids smiling." Monsignor Eberz died in 1991 and is buried in Mount Olivet Cemetery.

CANTATE OMNES PUBLICATIONS

Perhaps no greater effort was made in the 1950's than the publication of the *Cantate Omnes Hymnal*. The first mention of this project is in the minutes from a board meeting on May 8, 1948. Permission was given by then Bishop O'Hara to begin work on the hymnal. The prelate said:"I never discourage anyone who is willing to work." Pastors and musicians were surveyed for hymn titles to be included. The clergy received this letter:

> Reverend dear Father,
>
> We presume that in your experience as pastor or assistant in various parishes, you have recognized the lack of uniformity in the choice and singing of hymns. In order to bring about an improvement in this condition, Bishop O'Hara has given his whole-hearted approval and support to the proposed compilation of practical and worthy hymns for congregational and school use throughout the diocese.
>
> We are sending a letter to your organist requesting a suggested list of hymns. You will probably want to confer with your organist in making recommendations. If you, personally, have any helpful suggestions, they will be

most welcome, and will you please send them along to the chairman Rev. Henry S. Kawalec, 3233 Main St., Buffalo, 14, NY, or the secretary, Mrs. Cecelia R. Kenny, 159 York St., Buffalo 13, NY. An earnest effort is being made to produce this hymnal at a nominal cost so that it would be possible for you to supply enough copies in your Church for congregational use or, if preferred, each person could afford to purchase his own copy.

Thank you for your cooperation.

Sincerely yours,
Mrs. Cecelia Kenny

This project took five years before publication on the feast of the Assumption, 1952. William Keller, Inc. of Buffalo produced and lithographed the hymnal. It has been said that Bishop Burke christened the book with the title *Cantate Omnes* (*Sing Ye All*). Editors included Father Eberz, Father Kawalec, and Cecelia Kenny. Acknowledgment was made to the art department of Rosary Hill College and to others for their preparation of the copy for lithography. Sister Jeanne File, OSF, was founder and chair of the art department then. We do know that Cecelia Kenny's sisters helped. Father Paul Juenker and Father Raymond Liszka translated the Latin hymns into English. Father Matrin Marnon helped with editing of the texts, and Louis Huybrechts wrote some of the harmonizations. A supplement was added in 1958, and subsequent editions added more material in the 1960's.

Louis Huybrechts, who immigrated from Belgium, worked at Saint Louis Church from 1952 to 1954. He studied at the Lemmens Institute, Royal Conservatory of Music, and did graduate study under Flor Peeters, a renowned Flemish composer and organist. Louis published many compositions. He left the church over dissatisfaction about the rebuilding of the Kimball pipe organ at Saint Louis Church. He subsequently went to work briefly for Sacred Heart Cathedral in Rochester. Huybrechts later moved to Sacred Heart Church and Duquesne University, Pittsburgh, where he died in 1973.

The goal was to develop a hymnal with a sufficient number of hymns for all occasions and at a price within the means of every student. In 1954 the melody edition sold for thirty-five cents, with pre-paid orders amounting to $2000. The hymnal went to print and the diocese paid the deficit of $4300. In 1953, 200 hymnals were delivered to the Wende prison and a bonfire was created on June 10 to burn the old Saint Basil Hymnals! Two years later, the first printing of 25,000 copies was almost gone and the bishop was repaid. The hymnal was in general use throughout the diocese with copies also sold to military chaplains.

In 1953, Ted Marier, a well-known chant scholar, reviewed the hymnal in the *Cecelia* magazine, commenting on the hand drawn notes and felt that the low cost would help to sell the product. He did criticize, for whatever reason, the inclusion of "Faith of Our Fathers" which had direct reference to English Catholics enduring the Protestant Reformation.

In 1954 Msgr. Kawalec asked permission of Bishop Burke to print 10,000 more voice copies for the amount of $1992. He also asked permission to promote the sale of *Cantate Omnes* to Catholic school departments in other dioceses. Cecelia Kenny commented that "we worked for four years, compiling, editing and doing accompaniments for it before it was published in 1952. My sisters and many, many others helped with much of it, especially my sister Collette who printed much of the music by hand and hand copied much of the hymnal." The music book was the official hymnal of the United States Army Chaplains at one time. By 1960, there were 120,000 copies of the hymnal in print and 180,000 additional congregation participation aids were published. This author has seen editions with a copyright from 1952, 1958, and 1963.

In 1967 there was a significant departure in format. The hymnal was called *Community Mass,* including the propers for each Sunday and the canon of the Mass. The ordinary included an English version of Gregorian chant and the "Mass of Christian Unity" by Jan Vermulst. It is interesting to note that in the 1971 obituary of Jerome Murphy, the late diocesan director of music, it is stated that Murphy composed the *Cantate Omnes Hymnal.* There is no record of his contribution to the project.

THE CATHOLIC CHOIRMASTERS GUILD 1946–1964

As noted earlier, Sister Mary Grace began the Buffalo unit of the National Catholic Music Educators Association in 1944 under the superintendancy of Msgr. Sylvester Hoebel. Father Kawalec was the chairman and Cecelia Kenny served as secretary, but it soon became apparent that there was a need for a Catholic organists guild. On September 15, 1946, the National Catholic Music Educators Association met at Mount Saint Joseph Academy. The attendees made the decision that two organizations would exist: the Buffalo unit of the NCMEA and the Catholic Choirmasters Guild. The second Sunday of the month was set aside for meetings. On October 13, 1946, the first meeting of the newly organized Catholic Choirmasters Guild took place at Our Lady of Lourdes Church hall. Officers were elected: president Rev. Henry Kawalec, vice president Rev. Paul Valente, corresponding secretary Cecelia Kenny, recording secretary Mary Heinz, and treasurer Leonard Weiland. A choir of priests presented a music demonstration, and plans were formulated to offer chant classes at the Stella Niagara Normal School under the direction of Kawalec and Valente. Officers made plans to schedule a concert by Dr. Eugene Lapierre at Saint Joseph's Old Cathedral on November 14 of that same year. This was all accomplished in that first meeting! By May 1947, an umbrella organization entitled the Catholic Music Association was formed with three sub-divisions: NCMEA, the Catholic Choirmasters Guild, and the Diocesan Choir.

Big projects were developed such as the music festival at Kleinhan's Music Hall on March 2, 1947. Father Eberz directed choirs from the Little Seminary, Mount Saint Mary, Saint Mary Seminary, Immaculate Heart of Mary, and Mount Saint Joseph High Schools. John Surra conducted a 90-piece orchestra. Many people came to Buffalo to attend the Eucharistic Congress in September, 1948, and a choir of 500 was created to lead the singing at the opening mass in the War Memorial Stadium. Forty-two thousand people attended the event to commemorate the centennial of the creation of the Diocese of Buffalo.

In May 1946, a tradition was begun to host family-oriented socials for Guild members. The first one was held at Stella Niagara in May 1946. From 1950 to 1990, parishes alternated hosting the annual June gathering. In 1949, the liturgical commission for the Diocese of Buffalo was chaired by Monsignor John Weismantel with Fathers Bojacki, Eberz, Trevett, with Kawalec serving as secretary.

After the founding of Rosary Hill College, a liturgical music major for a bachelor's degree of 138 credits was established at the college in 1952. The enrollment for the first year yielded 26 students but lasted only two years. At that time, Sister Brendan and Ellen Kenny were running the department. The program included classes in chant, conducting, counterpoint, polyphony, liturgy and Latin. Cecelia Kenny, Jerome Murphy, Rev. Eberz and Msgr. Kawalec were instructors for the program, in addition to the regular music faculty of the college. According to Sister Georgia Dunn, the group teaching the program dropped the project because of a disagreement on the interpretation of the rhythm of chant. She said there were three points of view on this subject and a consensus could not be reached.

In 1953, commemoration was made of the 50th anniversary of the promulgation of the *Moto Proprio* of Pope Pius X. This document affected the work of Professor Singenberger and was a foundational guide to the publication of the diocesan music guidelines in 1956. A Mass of Thanksgiving was celebrated at Saint Joseph's Old Cathedral. Four hundred singers from 14 churches sang, accompanied by Cecelia on the historic Hook and Hastings pipe organ.

The Saint Pius X sub-chapter was created in 1954 for the southern tier area of the diocese. Established by Fathers Eberz and Valente, the sub-chapter lasted into the 1960's. For liturgical history buffs, it should be noted that the dialogue Mass began on November 27, 1958. This was a result of the liturgical movement that fostered the active participation of the assembly. However, the Mass remained in the Latin language.

The newsletter *Quilisma* began in September 1956 with Msgr. Kawalec as editor for the first year and Rev. Norman McLaughlin serving for the second year and was mailed to all people in the diocese who were interested in liturgical music. This policy was changed in 1965, and only Guild members received the newsletters with dues to be paid by October 1. Ethel Grabenstetter eventually became the editor beginning in 1958, continuing for more than thirty years while also serving as the organist at Blessed Trinity Church and as a school principal. A charter member of the Guild, Ethel was keenly interested in the liturgical movement, and she received the Saint Joseph the Worker award for her work. Robert Chambers described her as "vibrant." Msgr. Kawalec called her a "litnik," that is, someone who followed the liturgical movement enthusiastically. Ethel passed away in 1991. For some old timers in the Guild, carrying this liturgy stuff too far resulted in their departure from the organization and the nickname "litnik" was used with a negative connotation.

Sister Mary Grace developed the Junior Organist Guild in 1960. The goal was to prepare young organists to substitute during the summer. Classes began at Saint Mary Seminary with tests to be given in June. Those who passed satisfactorily received certificates.

Another milestone for the Buffalo musicians was to host the National

Catholic Music Educators Association conference at the Statler Hilton in 1960. Although not properly a Guild function, many Guild leaders participated in this affair. Sister Mary Grace and Sister Gertrude Mary, Sister Cuthbert, Sister Margaret of the Cross, and Rev. Norman McLaughlin chaired the elementary music education department presentations. A choral concert was given combining the college choirs directed by Cecelia Kenny, Robert Schultz, Rev. Michael Palotai, Gerard Reinagel, and Michael Slominski. Sister M. Raymond (Frances Roberts) presented a piano recital. Saint Mary of Sorrows Church Choir performed under the direction of Robert Schultz. Msgr. Kawalec gave an address entitled "Are We Making Adequate Provision for Future Church Musicians?" Cecelia Kenny conducted an elementary girls choir accompanied by Sister Corona. Sister M. Gloria (Gloria McLaughlin) presented a lecture on the use of television in the music curriculum. There was an organ recital at Saint Benedict's Church on the new Schlicker pipe organ. Sister Lorentine, Sister Corona, Sister Agnes, Sister Albert Ann (Mary Louise Franier), and Sister Carolino also provided leadership for the conference.

Robert Chambers served as Guild president in 1963 and 1969. He said that board meetings were often held at his home on the west side. Both he and Cecelia Kenny lived on York Street. The Guild was a very social organization with several social activities every year. Continuing education programs were held at downtown Stella Niagara Normal School on Washington Street during the summer. In 1962, the Second Vatican Council was convened by Pope John XXIII, lasting for four years with the goal of renewing the life of the Church. The first document of the Council was on the liturgy, *Sacrosanctum Concilium*. This decree had a broad impact, not only on the worship of the Roman Catholic Church, but also on liturgical reforms among the all Christian denominations.

CATHOLIC CHOIRMASTERS/CHURCH MUSICIANS GUILD 1965–1988

In 1964, most church musicians were in a panic as they had to prepare new music with English texts beginning with Advent. English propers were provided in the newsletter for immediate use; this included the introit, gradual, offertory, and communion verses.

In the minutes for the Guild board meeting during the summer of 1975, members discussed the need to incorporate diverse liturgical ministers into the Guild. It was thought that the name Catholic Choirmasters discouraged folk musicians, instrumentalists, cantors, and song leaders from joining the organization. Under the leadership of Paul Golden, president, and Msgr. Kawalec, moderator, the board decided to change the Guild's constitution to reflect the broader constituency. Therefore, the name of the organization was changed to the Church Musicians Guild of Buffalo and the title of the newsletter was changed to *The Church Musician*. The last issue of *Quilisma* was issued in November 1975. Subsequently, the board began the process to affiliate with the new national organization, the National Association of Pastoral Musicians (NPM). This organization was founded in 1976 by Rev. Virgil Funk after the National Catholic Music Educators Association ceased to operate.

Virgil Funk wrote David Nease in December 1982 to discuss a possible affiliation, dues reimbursement, and Buffalo's offer to host a regional convention. On July 20, 1983, Funk wrote again to Nease to discuss modifications to the NPM by-laws in order to incorporate the Guild as a pre-existing member. Such changes involved the name of the chapter, application fee, and modifying the national by-laws in order to respect the local unit's traditions, as well as the need for a statement signed by the Bishop of Buffalo approving the affiliation. The first charter of the Buffalo, New York, chapter of NPM was granted in August 1983, along with the signature of the two leaders, David Nease and Virgil Funk.

David Nease remembers that "both the CMG and NPM were concerned about maintaining the integrity of each organization. At the time, NPM was still forming its identity while CMG was a well-established group. I believe that CMG initiated the conversation and Father Virgil Funk, founder and president of NPM, personally traveled to Buffalo to discuss our becoming a chapter, while maintaining our heritage. He was always very supportive of CMG and, as I mentioned, he attended our 50th anniversary liturgy and dinner in 1996." Sister Judith Kubicki said that this process began during her presidency and concluded under David Nease's administration.

In 1992, NPM presented the Church Musicians Guild with the chapter of the year award. Virgil Funk, president, wrote on June 17 of that year that the award was given for "the extensive longevity of the Buffalo Guild as well as the outstanding service to the work of the association since becoming a chapter...providing an excellent model for other dioceses to follow." Sister Judith Kubicki accepted the award from Richard Gibila at the NPM convention in Philadelphia at the members' breakfast. At the same time, the Pastoral Musician of the Year award was presented to Rev. Lucien Deiss. The plaque was inscribed with the following:

1992 NPM Outstanding

Chapter of the Year Award

Presented to

Buffalo Guild of Musicians

for modeling

how the old can blend with the new,

how the young can lead the old,

how unity is possible in diversity.

NPM Regional Convention 1988

David Nease maintained that he would never have been able to put together the convention without the help of many people. About 625 people attended the event. The theme of the regional NPM conference was "Transformed through Excellence." The event was held on July 18-21, 1988. Major presenters were Rev. Edward Foley, OFM Cap., Sister Cynthia Serjak, RSM, John-Michael Caprio, Rev. William Bauman, and Rev. Virgil Funk, president of NPM. Dr. Fred Moleck led the hymn festival. Bishop Edward Head presided at the Eucharist, and Don Fellows directed the music for the service. Many remember the processional hymn that Rev. Michael Joncas wrote for the Guild's 40th anniversary which was used again for the convention: "I Will Go Up to the Altar of God," scored for choir and organ. The handwritten score is located in the archives and includes movements for the Rite of Sprinkling and the Gloria. Most events were held in the Hyatt Regency Hotel with some meetings at Saint Joseph Cathedral, Saint Paul Cathedral, the Hilton Hotel, and the Buffalo Convention Center. The core committee consisted of David Nease, chairman, Donald Fellows, Sister Judith Marie Kubicki, Rev. Jacob Ledwon, Patricia Otis, with Rev. Edward Grosz, *ex officio.*

NPM ORGAN SCHOOL

Buffalo had the opportunity to host the NPM Organ School from June 26-30,1995. The program was held on the campus of the State University College at Fredonia. Instructors included Dr. James Kosnik, Dr. John Hofmann, Sister Mary Jane Wagner, and Father Ronald Rebaldo. The theme of the seminar was "Leading the Assembly from the Organ." About 24 people participated in the program which incorporated an organ crawl organized by Alan Lukas. Regina Doherty was most enthusiastic about her experience. "We had the best of everything…we were treated so well, not as students, but as peers…how great it was losing sleep for study, pray and play with no distractions, with others, from near and far, who love the work they do. We received outlines and bibliographic handouts at each session…the program was for everyone, regardless of skill level."

50TH ANNIVERSARY OF THE CHURCH MUSICIANS GUILD

The Guild planned many activities to celebrate the golden jubilee of the organization in 1996. The opening event was Solemn Vespers on Sunday, August 11, at Holy Cross Church. Dr. James Kosnik played the organ for the service.

September 22 was the date for the homecoming celebration for former, current, and honorary members of the organization, hosted by All Saints Church. Former resident Don Fellows gave an organ recital with Alan Lukas leading hymns for congregational singing.

Bishop Mansell celebrated Mass at Saint Joseph's Cathedral on November 17. Ron Martin directed the jubilee choir with Patrick Barrett, Alan Lukas, and Gail Shepherd assisting. The service opened with the composition "I Will Go Up" by Michael Joncas, commissioned by the Guild for its 40th anniversary. Anthems included "Sing to the Lord a New Song" by Ron Martin and *"Adoremus In Aeternum"* by Gregorio Allegri. Sister Judith Kubicki and Robert Chambers served as lectors, Harold Harden, Jeffrey Porter, and Jean Marie Stackpoole cantored. The service was also supported by a brass ensemble.

The banquet, held after the service at the Buffalo Hilton at the Waterfront, honored guest Rev. Virgil Funk, the founder and president of the National Association of Pastoral Musicians. David Nease remembers that hundreds of people attended the celebration, including many clergy. Over 150 people were present for the banquet. Dinner tickets included a copy of the Guild history booklet.

The jubilee year climaxed with a choral concert on Friday May 10, 1996. Frank Scinta conducted the festival choir which sang Mozart's "*Ave Verum*" and Ralph Vaughan Williams' "O Clap Your Hands." The 300 singers celebrated the anniversary including the choirs from All Saints, Blessed Trinity, Blessed Sacrament, Fourteen Holy Helpers, Holy Family, Our Lady of Victory, Queen of Martyrs, Saint Amelia, Saint Bonaventure, Saint Gabriel, and Saint John the Baptist (Kenmore). David Nease chaired the event, and Patrick Barrett accompanied the choir. With the observance of the jubilee, Ernestine Otis retired as historian for the Guild. She had been a member since 1955 and took great pride in documenting the history of the Guild.

21st Century: Adapting to the New Normal

By the 21st century the Guild had changed considerably, since most of the pioneer leaders of the Guild had died by 1995, including lay leaders Ethel Grabenstetter and Ernestine Otis, both very active in the Guild, as well as Msgr. Kawalec, Msgr. Eberz, and Sister Ryan. In 2007-2008, the "Journey of Faith and Grace" initiated a process by which many parishes were closed or merged because of declining attendance and fewer priests available to staff the parishes. In 1965 the Diocese of Buffalo had staffed 268 parishes with 1,194 priests (diocesan and religious) and 3,417 sisters. As of 2018, that number has declined significantly. The Diocese has 364 priests, 145 deacons, and 638 sisters who serve 161 parishes, but many of these priests and religious are retired or semi-retired. At one time, the area comprising the Diocese of Buffalo was 50% Catholic. Today the change in demographics has reduced the Catholic population to 44% of the people in western New York.

The declining number of parishes required a reduced number of liturgical musicians serving those parishes. The earliest record for Guild membership is from 1960 with a list of over 150 members. By 1978, the enrollment reached a high of over 200 members. The 1986 directory listed 183 names as members. As of 2018, the Guild has 115 members. Nevertheless, the Church Musicians Guild maintains the distinction of being the oldest continuous organization of Catholic Church musicians in the United

States. Despite the decline in the number of parishes and personnel, there have been many bright lights shining as a result of the skills and talents of people who have earned a national reputation in liturgy or liturgical music.

Our own Bishop Edward Grosz is a native of Assumption Church in Buffalo. He distinguished himself by earning an MA in Liturgical Studies at the University of Notre Dame. The bishop headed our Office of Worship for many years. Now that he is an auxiliary bishop, he no longer is able to do such work, yet continues to support our parish musicians with thoughtful letters of encouragement. The bishop chaired the committee that wrote the document "Sing to the Lord," published in 2007 for the American Church. This text is the working bible for all church musicians and has received good reviews from all experts in the field. Bishop Grosz worked with other bishops on the sub-committee for Music in the Liturgy for the Bishops Committee on the Liturgy. Advisors to the group included experts such as Leo Nestor (deceased) from Catholic University of America, Robert Batastini (retired) from GIA Publications, John Foley, SJ, of Saint Louis University, Michael McMahon, formerly president of National Association of Pastoral Musicians, and Anthony Ruff, OSB, from Saint John's University in Minnesota.

Sister Judith Kubicki is well-known in the United States as professor of liturgical theology at Fordham University in New York City. A member of the Felician Sisters, she earned a master's in English from Canisius College, a Master of Liturgical Music from Catholic University of America, and a PhD in Liturgical Studies also from Catholic University. Kubicki was formerly president of the North American Academy of Liturgy and writes for journals such as *Worship, GIA Quarterly* and has authored several books. Her current research focuses on the topic of hymn texts. *The Song of the Singing Assembly: A Theology of Christian Hymnody* was published in 2017 by GIA Publications. Sister Judith received the Jubilate Deo award from

NPM in 2019. She credits this recognition of her lifelong work as having begun with her involvement in the Church Musicians Guild. She said that she first became acquainted with the Guild while serving as chauffeur for Sisters Evangeline and Martinelle who attended Guild meetings faithfully.

Dr. James Kosnik grew up in Assumption parish in the Black Rock area of Buffalo, and he began working as a musician in his home parish in 1963. The pastor, Msgr. Maximillian Bogacki,

"took me under his guidance. I was payed $1.00 per weekday mass and $3.00 per Sunday mass with the proviso by Msgr. Bogacki that I would use part of my salary to seek out an organ teacher (who was Don Ingram from St. Paul's Cathedral) and a voice teacher (Marie Mohr) and my father would replace my current piano teacher with August Martin, of the piano faculty at SUNY (Buffalo). In 1966 I became a member of the Buffalo Church Musicians Guild. My conversion to pastoral music occurred quickly when I was introduced to workshops and concerts by renowned musicians like C. Alexander Peloquin and Sister Theophane Hytrek. My conviction was that I wanted to follow their passion and achievement in sacred music at the highest level."

Kosnik earned an MA in music history from SUNY Buffalo and a doctorate in organ performance in 1979 from the Eastman School of Music of the University of Rochester. For a number of years, Kosnik worked in our diocese at Saint Joseph Cathedral, Christ the King Seminary, and Villa Maria College. For over 35 years, he taught at Old Dominion University in Virginia where he is still employed. Kosnik has distinguished himself with performances all over the world including the Vatican and Harvard University, published or edited numerous organ compositions, and taught for the National Association of Pastoral Musicians at organ schools and national conventions.

The Guild has been honored by the continuing membership of Donald

Fellows of Saint Paul's Cathedral, Pittsburgh. He was a master's graduate of State University College at Fredonia and served as music director of Saint Joseph Cathedral. Fellows moved on to the Ogdensburg cathedral and then to the Chicago cathedral where he assisted music director Richard Proulx. Now a resident of Pittsburgh, Fellows plays the nationally renowned von Beckerath pipe organ, installed under the musical leadership of Paul Koch (John Singenberger's grandson). The music director has been in this position since 1999.

Joel Kumro is a young musician who has distinguished himself since he left Buffalo. Kumro is a singer/organist who graduated from Saint John's University, Minnesota, with a master's degree in liturgical music. He is now stationed at Saint Benedict Church in Richmond, Virginia. On the national level, Kumro is remembered for winning the Kosnik scholarship through NPM. Kumro gained board experience by membership on the boards of the Guild, the Buffalo Philharmonic Chorus, and the NPM committee for chapters and organists.

Many Guild members recall Carl Johengen, a respected singer and nationally known composer. Johengen earned his doctorate in voice from Eastman School of Music and taught at several colleges in the state. He served as director of music for the Diocese of Syracuse. Now a resident of Bath, New York, he is best known as a composer. His *Veni Creator Spiritus* was premiered before a large audience at NPM and won first place in a contest sponsored by World Library Publications. His work is published by World Library, Selah, GIA, and Hope.

Another bright light came from North Tonawanda. John Kubiniec left our area to study at Saint Joseph College, Indiana, and Colgate Rochester Divinity School where he earned his Master of Divinity. He is credited with helping to start the Rochester NPM chapter. After working as a pastoral musician in New York City, Kubiniec has retired to a part-time position at

Gates Presbyterian Church near Rochester so he can have more time as a quilter.

A native of Buffalo, Kathy Felong made her mark in the Diocese of Erie as music director of Holy Cross parish of Fairview, Pennsylvania, where she leads a contemporary ensemble. After earning a master's degree in liturgy from the University of Notre Dame, Felong has helped NPM raise money for the Mark C. Kulyk fund. Previously she co-authored *Beyond Strumming* with NPM president Steve Petrunak. Felong currently serves as editor of *Pastoral Music*, the magazine published by NPM.

The Guild has moved to align itself more closely with the National Association of Pastoral Musicians guidelines. The new national by-laws have suggested ex-officio positions and term limits for officers who now have to be members of the national organization. Retirees pay half of the membership fee, similar to the NPM fee structure.

We members of the Guild have responded to the electronic age with the development of our website, Facebook page, and use of emails to members. The board insures contact with members through surveys utilized to gauge the opinions of Guild members. Our organization has also continued to cooperate with the Buffalo chapter of the American Guild of Organists in sponsoring organ recitals and choral workshops.

On the cusp of the 75th anniversary of the foundation of the Guild, this organization hopes to achieve its centennial in 2046. Liturgy and music work hand in hand with the dedicated members of the Guild to communicate what words alone cannot express. Whether we are volunteer or salaried, degreed or self-taught, there is a mutual respect among our members as we seek the same goal: to love God, serve the Church, and lead the assembly in prayerful song.

EPILOGUE

Where do we go from here? If we look at the goals that the original Cecilians espoused, we have accomplished some but not all of their objectives. We have established congregational singing as the norm, but have moved beyond chant and polyphony to many musical styles in the vernacular. As we have become sensitive to issues of diversity and multiculturalism, we have broadened our repertoire in both styles of music and the languages in which we sing. Nor is the organ the only instrument utilized in worship today. The legalism of the "White List" of the 1950's which prohibited certain musical selections has been replaced by a conceptual framework in which the musical, pastoral, and liturgical judgements are considered equally. It is a tall order to develop skills in pastoral musicians who can teach chant, Hispanic melodies, gospel, spirituals, and the newly developed praise and worship music. The greatest challenge to musicians today might be to incorporate new forms of music in balance with our European heritage.

For the Church Musicians Guild of Buffalo, the challenge remains of how to make music normative in our worship. For some church members raised before Vatican II, the liturgy is essentially a spoken service dominated by the priest. In the twenty-first century, we have seen a lost generation of millennials who need to be brought back into the fold. It was the advocacy of Cecilian movement that led to the 1956 document issued by the Diocese of Buffalo. Based on the "White List," reforms were made to centralize liturgical music directives. Under the tutelage of John Singenberger, those principles and skills were brought to Buffalo by Leo Roy. Cecelia and her sisters promoted the movement through the publication of *Cantata Omnes* publications for congregational singing. Sister Mary Grace Ryan continued the education of musicians by helping to form the local unit of the NCMEA and by directing the junior organists training program. Kawalec brought Solemnes chant standards to the Diocese and used his clerical position to promote liturgical music ministry. Eberz served in a supporting role to these endeavors primarily through the direction of the priests choir.

With gratitude to our pioneers, let us move forward to promote the Gospel in song!

ACKNOWLEDGMENTS

I wish to acknowledge the help and courtesy of Kathleen Delany, archivist of Canisius College. Through the intervention of Sarah Sutcliffe, our small collection was accepted into the library of Canisius College. During my many visits there to seek information about the Guild, Kathleen was most helpful and taught me archival procedures. The Guild deeply appreciates the hospitality of Canisius College in housing our historical memorabilia in the local history division of the library.

The author thanks Dr. James Estep, Dr. James Kosnik and David Nease, who read the manuscript and offered suggestions to improve the document.

I wish to thank editor, Dr. Monica Weis, SSJ, a retired professor of English at Nazareth College, published author, and a talented musician. I am grateful for her interest in this project and her willingness to read a document penned by a novice writer. I have known Sister Monica since 1965 when I was her student, and she was my sixth grade teacher!

I offer a big thank you to Eileen Roy, granddaughter of Leo and Magdelena Roy, for sharing her collection of family memorabilia. The photographs of her grandparents and Aunt Cecilia are published in this document due to her generosity.

I wish to acknowledge the help of Michael Riester, the archivist of Saint Louis Church. Mike participated and recorded the oral histories given by Msgr. Paul Juenker, Joseph Rozler, and Robert Chambers.

Appendix A – Awards

50+ year membership awards

2014 David Nease, Maria Smith, Mary Jane Mescall

2015 Eleanor Asklar

2016 James Kosnik, Edward Witul, Robert Winkler

2017 Sister Judith Kubicki

2019 Regina Doherty

2020 Frank Scinta

Cecilia Roy Kenny Award

1982 St. Andrew's Church, Kenmore

2014 Bridget Dick

2015 Eleanor Asklar

2016 Gail Shepherd

2017 David Nease

2018 Robert Chambers

2019 Frank Scinta

Liturgical Music Award for Youth Adults

2018 Chelsea Brodka

2019 Victoria Erdman

APPENDIX B – BOARD OF DIRECTORS 2019-2020

Church Musicians Guild of Buffalo

Board of Directors 2019-2020

Bill Fay, newsletter editor

Peter Gonciarz, programming coordinator

Michael Hauser, treasurer

Joseph Morreal, hospitality

Maria Chomicka, secretary

Heather Lovelace, webmistress

Robert Kiercz, registrar

Members at Large: Sarah Rice

Edward Witul

Chelsea Brodka

Ex- officio: Bill Fay, past director

Alan Lukas, diocesan director of music

Rev. John Mack, chaplain

APPENDIX C – PRESIDENTS/DIRECTORS

Presidents (Directors) of Church Musicians Guild (approximate)

1946 Msgr. Henry Kawalec

1948 Joseph Keller

1950 Joseph Keller

1953 Cecelia Roy Kenny

1956 Rev. Christian Puehn

1957 Rev. Paul Eberz

1959 Ethel Grabenstetter

1961 Joseph Keller

1963 Robert Chambers

1965 Robert Allen

1967 Bernice Baldwin

1969 Robert Chambers

1971 Rev. Louis Dolinic

1973 Edward Witul

1975 Paul Golden

1977 James Kosnik

1979 Sister Judith Kubicki

1981 David Nease

1984 Alan Lukas

1986 Rev. Jacob Ledwon

1988 Patricia Otis

1990 Donald Fellows

1991 Sister Judith Kubicki

1993 David Nease

1998 Alan Lukas

2000 Alan Lukas

2002 Gail Shepherd

2004 Gail Shepherd

2006 Rev.Jeff Nowak

20008 Rev. Jeff Nowak

2008 Gail Shepherd

2010 Ed Witul

2012 Gail Shepherd

2013 Bill Fay

2015 BIll Fay

2017 Bill Fay

2019 Bill Fay (past director)

Appendix D – Moderators

Moderators

Msgr .Henry Kawalec 1950-1977

Rev. Louis Dolinic 1978-1984

Rev. Paul Bossi 1984-2008

Rev. John Mack 2008-

APPENDIX E – ORGAN SCHOLARSHIP WINNERS

Organ Scholarship Winners

1989 Joel Warden

1991 Gregory Wagner

1992 Barbara Siracuse

1993 Linda Shoemaker

1994 Thomas Rogers

1995 Cynthia Margaret Stotz

1996 Emese Tredo

1997 Jonathan Szematowicz

1998 Kevin Durkin & Phillip Revekant

1999 Stephanie Ann Waodowski

2000 Joseph Dietterich & Catherine Ann Kiercz

2001 John Myers

2002 William Weiss

2003 Jason Baer

2004 Bradley Wingert

2005 Peter Gonciarz

2009 Daniel Pisarcik

2010 Peter Gonciarz and Joel Kumro

2011 William Freeman

2012 Nick Del Bello and Lorenzo Quebral

2013 Amelia Wroblewski

2014 no auditions

2015 Maria Chomicka

2016 Maria Chomicka & Matthew Caputy

2017 Matthew Caputy

2018 James Bobak

2019 James Boback

Appendix F – Convention Speakers

Guest Recitalists and Speakers (incomplete)

1946 Dr. Eugene Lapierre at Old Cathedral

1947 Rev Ermin Vitry, Dr. Clifford Bennet

1948 Conrad Bernier at New Cathedral

1949 Mario Salvador at Old Cathedral

1950 Flor Peeters at Old Cathedral

1951 Mario Salvador at Old Cathedral

1953 John Selner SS, Rev Clifford Howell SJ

1954 Louis Huybrechts at Saint Benedict's Church

1955 Rev Michael Palotoi S.P.

1957 Rev John Selner

1961 Vincent Higginson

1962 Rev. Clifford Howell SJ

1964 Roger Wagner

1966 C. Alexander Peloquin, Donald Ingram

1969 C Alexander Peloquin, Frederick Burgomaster

1970 Rev. Joseph Champlain

1971 Cherry Rhodes at St. John Vianney Seminary

1973 C. Alexander Peloquin

1974 James Kosnik at Christ the King Seminary

1975 Peter Hurford at St Paul's Cathedral

1977 Dr. Kim Kasling at St Joseph's Cathedral

1978 John Stowe at Christ the King Seminary

1979 Alexander Peloquin, Thomas Murray

1980 The Dameans

1981 Robert Batastini, Joanne jasinksi

1982 Sister Theophane Hytrek, Michael Joncas

1984 Rev. Patrick Collins

1985 Charles Callahan

1986 David Haas, Sistine Chapel Choir

1990 Rev. John Gallen SJ

1991 Rev. John Gallen SJ

1992 Sister Cynthia Serjak RSM

1993 Gabe Huck

1994 Dr. Fred Molek

1995 Rev. Michael Joncas

1996 Alice Parker

1997 Dr. Elaine Rendler

1998 Dr. Fred Moleck

1999 Rev. Richard Fragomeni

2000 Rev. Richard Fragomeni

2001 Richard Proulx

2002 Jim Hansen & Melanie Coddington

2003 Rev. James Chepponis

2004 Sister Delores Dufner OSB

2005 Peter Ghiloni

2006 Rev. Michael Joncas

2007 Bob Hurd

2008 John Angotti

2009 Steven Janco

2010 Marty Haugen, Rev. Michael Joncas & Tony Alonso

2011 Bishop Edward Grosz

2012 Steven Warner

20013 Rev. MIchael Driscoll

2015 Sister Judith Kubicki

2017 Rev. Ricky Manalo

2020 Dr. J.J. Wright

APPENDIX G – GUILD MEMBERS 1986

Guild Members 1986

Robert Allen, Assumption, Buffalo

Sister M. Barbara Amrozowicz, Our Lady of Loretto, Buffalo

Frances Anzalone, Holy Spirit, North Collins

Petrina Arroyo, St. Stephen, Buffalo

Mrs. Eugene Asklar, Our Lady of Mount Carmel, Niagara Falls

Bernice Baldwin, sub organist

Anna Mae Balmas, St. Mary, Silver Springs

Mrs. Arthur Barber, honorary

Ms. Betty Barna, St. Mark, Kendall

Louella Barre, St. Joseph, Batavia

Patrick Barrett, Fourteen Holy Helpers, West Seneca

Robert Bastastini, GIA Publications, Chicago

Marie Baumgarten, honorary

Joan Benz, St. Martin, Buffalo

Rev. Joseph Bissonette, St. Bartholomew, Buffalo

Rev. Paul Bossi, Holy Cross, Buffalo

Patricia Bradfuhrer, Blessed Sacrament, Tonawanda

Dianne Braun, Holy Spirit, Buffalo

Gertrude Brenner, honorary

Richard Brooks, Most Holy Redeemer, Buffalo

Barbara Brown,St. John Vianney, Orchard Park

Jane Brown, St. Amelia, Tonawanda

Ralph Brownscheidle, honorary

George Buckenmeyer, St. Joseph, Batavia

Kathy Busmire, St. Mark, Kendall

Frank Cannata, St .Stephen, Grand Island

Nancy Cannizzaro, Holy Cross, Buffalo

Eleanor Chadwick, St. Joseph, Albion

Robert Chambers, Holy Angels, Buffalo

Rita Chatley, honorary

Julie Ciesinski, St. Thomas Aquinas, Buffalo

Mrs. James Codd, honorary

Robert Colby, Delaware Organ Company, Tonawanda

Audrey Coursen, honorary

Sister Mary Damien, Cattaraugus

Therese Daul, St. Martin, Buffalo

Joseph Dentino, St. Gabriel, Elma

Dennis DePerro, Holy Family, Buffalo

John DiPasquale, Our Lady of Victory, Lackawanna

Jackie Dippert, Immaculate Conception, East Aurora

Rev. Gregory Dobson, Our Lady of the Blessed Sacrament, Depew

Regina Doherty, St. Martin, Buffalo

Rev. Louis Dolinic, Our Lady of Czestochowa, North Tonawanda

Robert Dombrowski, F Clef Quartet, Buffalo

Kathy Donahue, honorary

Msgr. Paul Eberz, honorary

Rev. Benedict Ehmann, Rochester

Msgr. Francis Engler, St. Rose of Lima, Buffalo

Donald Fellows, St. Joseph Cathedral, Buffalo

Linda Frost, St. John the Baptist, Alden

Rev. Virgil Funk, NPM, Washington, D.C.

Joseph Gabalski, Our Lady of Czestochowa, North Tonawanda

Norma Gaiser, Holy Name of Jesus, Buffalo

Wallace Gardon, Holy Apostles, SS. Peter and Paul, Buffalo

John Giles, Our Lady of Perpetual Help, Lakeview

Joyce Gilroy, St. Mary of the Angels, Olean

Lisa Gortzig, St. Martin, Buffalo

Ethel Grabenstetter, Blessed Trinity, Buffalo

Sister Mary Grace, honorary

Rev. Edward Grosz, Office of Worship, Buffalo

Frank Guiliani -Giancola, Sacred Heart, Niagara Falls

Sheila Hamilton, St. Patrick, Salamanca

Anne Hart, St .Gerard, Buffalo

Evonne Hennebery, Holy Trinity, Dunkirk

Margery Hill,St. Mary of the Lake, Hamburg

Cecelia Howard,honorary

Sister Jane Huber, Stella Niagara Motherhouse, Stella Niagara

Glenn Hufnagel, Our Lady of Lourdes, Buffalo

Trudy Hughes, St. Mary, Holley

Dawn Jedrzejewski, St. Agnes, Buffalo

Helen Jordan, honorary

Msgr. Henry Kawalec, Assumption, Buffalo

Basil Kern, Immaculate Conception, Eden

Mary Jane Kersten, St. Aloysius, Cheektowaga

Robert Kiercz, Nativity of Our Lord, Orchard Park

Sister Mary Sheila Kimmit, St. John, Jamestown

Marie Knab

Mrs. Jerome Koch

Agnes Kopra, Blessed Trinity, Buffalo

Sister Virginia Kozlowski, Villa Maria Convent, Buffalo

Sister Judith Marie Kubicki,

Anthony Kunz, SS. Peter and Paul, Williamsville

Lenore Lambert, St. Benedict, Eggertsville

Rev. Jacob Ledwon, St. Joseph's Cathedral

Rev. John Leising, St. John the Baptist, Kenmore

Robert Levulis, Immaculate Conception, East Aurora

Margaret Littlefield, honorary

Rev. Paul Litwin, Nativity of Our Lord, Orchard Park

Alan Lukas, St. Andrew, Kenmore

Doris Lupp, St. Rose of Lima, Buffalo

Rev. Robert Mack, St. Francis Xavier, Buffalo

Albert Maggioli, St. Joseph, Buffalo

Victoria Maggioli, St. Joseph, Buffalo

Lawrence Maguda, St.Adalbert, Buffalo

Edward Makus, St. Hyacinth, Dunkirk

Ann Maloney,honorary

Lillian Maloney, honorary

Ann Marino, honorary

Mary Matteson, St. John Bosco, Sheridan

Anna Mayer, St. Isidore, East Otto

Rev. Leo McCarthy, St. Matthew, Buffalo

Jean Marie McCarthy, St .Patrick, Lockport

Mrs .R.J. McFarland, honorary

Rachel McGarrity, St. Anthony, Farnham

Mrs. James Mead, St. Cecelia, Oakfield

Roberta Meister, St. Amelia, Tonawanda

Mary Jane Mescall, Our Lady of the Blessed Sacrament, Depew

Joyce Michals, Immaculate Conception, East Aurora

Peter Miller, St. Joseph, Fredonia

Mary Mischka, Our Lady of Victory, Lackawanna

Catherine Miskuly, honorary

Rosella Morgano, Our Lady of Mount Carmel, Brant

Joan Mullhaupt, St. Joseph Cathedral, Buffalo

Timothy Mullhaupt, St. Joseph Cathedral, Buffalo

Philip Mure, St. Mark, Buffalo

Nels Muszynski, honorary

Ruth Myers, St. Patrick, Wheatville

David Nease, Our Lady of Victory, Lackawanna

Newman Apostolate, Erie Community College North, Williamsville

Eileen O'Brien, sub organist

Mary Beth Orlando, St. John the Baptist, Lockport

Ernestine Otis, sub organist

Patricia Otis, St. Edmund, Tonawanda

Angela Panepento, St. Margaret, Buffalo

Howard Penny, Sacred Heart, Bowmanville

Kevin Phalen, St. Gerard, Buffalo

Sister Eileen Pinkel, St. Mary of the Angels Convent, Williamsville

John Piscitello, Transfiguration, Buffalo

Marian Poland, St. Joseph, Fredonia

Dorothy Rebman, honorary

Dorthea Reilly, St. Joseph, Fredonia

Sister M. Esther Rellinger, Annunciation, Buffalo

Marnie Rozler, St. Mary of the Assumption, Lancaster

Jean Ruchalski, St. John the Baptist, Boston

Isabelle Russell, honorary

Robert Ryan, St. Bartholomew, Buffalo

Ruth Ryan, honorary

Rev. Robert Rybrczyk, St. Mary of the Angels, Olean

Suzanne Schneider, St. Joseph, North Tonawanda

David Schupp, St. Mary, Swormville

Suzanne Schwartz, St. Catherine of Siena, West Seneca

Frank Scinta, Blessed Sacrament, Buffalo

Mrs. Fran Seitz, honorary

Nancy Shaw, St. Francis of Assisi, Tonawanda

Gail Shepherd, SS. Peter and Paul, Hamburg

Irene Sielski, Queen of Peace, Buffalo

Judith Skretny, St. William, West Seneca

Peggy Slavin

Michael Slominski, honorary

Helene Smith

Maria Smith, St. Edmund, Tonawanda

Wayne Spencer, St. George, Westfall

Rev. Paul Steller, Newman Center, Erie Community College North

Norma Stetter, St. Agnes, Buffalo

Rev. William Stillwell, St. Mary of the Cataract, Niagara Falls

Rev. James Streng, Sacred Heart, Niagara Falls,

Marguerite Sullivan, St. Mary, Batavia

Ann Suozzi

Daniel Tenerowicz, Holy Mother of the Rosary Cathedral, Buffalo

Laurie Tramuta, Newman Center @ SUNY, Fredonia

Darlene Turzillo, Our Lady of Mount Carmel, Silver Creek

Sister Mary Ellen Twist, Sisters of Mercy Generalate, Orchard Park

Maria Tyksinski, St. Paul, Kenmore

Beverly Voll, Our Lady of the Blessed Sacrament, Depew

David Wagner, Christ the King, Snyder

Rev. James Wall, St. Joseph, Fredonia

Veronica Walters, honorary

Gloria Warchol, Mother of Divine Grace, Cheektowaga

Thomas Wenhold, St. Joseph, Lyndonville

Sister M. Emiliette Wernowski, Villa Maria Convent, Buffalo

Rev. Charles Werth, St. Joseph Buffalo

Tom Wilson, NPM, Washington, D.C.

Robert Winkler, St. Joseph, Buffalo

Dolores Witter, Sacred Heart, Portville

Edward Witul, St. Amelia, Tonawanda

Cheryl Wolner, St. Mary Holley

Msgr. Rupert Wright, St. Amelia, Tonawanda

Amanda Wurzer, honorary

Dorothy Young, honorary

Samuel Zalacca, St. Joseph, Leroy

Mrs. Walter Zale, honorary

Helen Zawadski, honorary

Mary Zeinz, honorary

BIBLIOGRAPHY

Bossi, Paul. "A Remembrance of Msgr. Paul Eberz." *The Church Musician,* 1992.

Carroll, Catherine. *A History of the Pius X School of Liturgical Music, 1916-1969.* St. Louis, MO: Society of the Sacred Heart,1989.

Carroll, Paul. "Leader in Church Race Relations, Monsignor Ebert Set to Retire." *Buffalo News,* December 18, 1982.

Catholic Normal School and Pio Nono College, Saint Francis. Catholic Church in Wisconsin.

Chambers, Robert. Interview by Bill Fay and Michael Riester, July 1, 2018.

Chepponis, James, Fred Moleck, and Cynthia Serjak. *From Organist to Pastoral Musician: A History of Church Music in the Catholic Diocese of Pittsburgh 1843-2006.* Pittsburgh PA: Catholic Diocese of Pittsburgh, 2006.

"Church Music Regulations for the Diocese of Buffalo." The Chancery, 1956.

"Church Organist Quits after 46 Years of Service." *Buffalo News,* October 27, 1954.

Crump Jean. "Music Hath Its Charm - Especially for the Roy Family." *WNY Catholic,* August 6, 1978.

Damien, Ronald. "A Historical Study of the Caecilian Movement in the United States." DMA diss., Catholic University of America, Washington DC,1984.

Dolonic, Rev. Louis. "Hands Praying and Playing: Life Reflections of a Priest-Musician." 2014.

Dunn, Georgia. *Hillsides: A Memoir*. Staten Island, NY: Society of Saint Paul, 1973.

Eberz, Paul. "Priests' Biographical Questionnaire." 1987.

Ellinwood, Leonard .*The History of American Church Music*. New York NY: L. Morehouse-Gorham Company, 1953.

Foley, Edward. *A Lyric Vision: The Music Documents of the US Bishops.* Collegeville MN: The Liturgical Press, 2009.

Foley, Edward. *Worship Music: A Concise Dictionary*. Collegeville MN: The Liturgical Press, 2000.

Foy, Felician. *1964 National Catholic Almanac*. Patterson, NJ: St. Anthony's Guild, 1964.

Fruchtbaum, Sue. "She Pilots Church Organ Today, but Woman Flier of the 30's Still Has Her Eyes on the Skies." *Buffalo Evening News*, June 23, 1967. (from the collection of the Buffalo History Museum.)

Ganz, Carl. *The Catholic Historian's Handbook Research and Writing Your First American Catholic History Project*. New Jersey Catholic Historical Commission, 2015.

Golden Jubilee of Catholic Normal School and Pio Nono College. Catholic Normal School, St. Francis WI, 1920.

Gorman Patrick , *An Analysis of the Choral Music of John Singenberger as It Relates to the Musical Philosophies of the Caecilian Movement.* University of Wisconsin-Madison. 1994.

Grabian, Bernadette. "Milwaukee Wisconsin: America's Nucleus of the St. Cecelia Society." *Sacred Music*, Volume 100, Issue 1, Spring 1973.

Gray, Sharon Lee. *A History of the National Catholic Music Educators Association 1942-1976*. University of Cincinnati, 1988.

Higginson, J. Vincent. *History of American Catholic Hymnals: Survey and Background.* The Hymn Society of America, 1982.

"J.T Murphy Dies; Was Music Director of Buffalo Diocese." *Buffalo Evening News*, November 3, 1971.

Joncas, Jan Michael. *From Sacred Song to Ritual Music: Twentieth Century Understanding of Worship Music.* Collegeville MN: Liturgical Press, 1997.

Kenny, Cecelia Roy. "From Cockpit to Console." (from the collection of the Buffalo History Museum.)

Kenny, Cecelia Roy. "The Status of Church Music in the Diocese of Buffalo." *Cecilia*, Volume 81 #5, 1954.

Kobielski, Milton, ed. Millennium of Christianity of the Polish People 966-1966: Buffalo Diocesan
Observance. Millennium Committee of the Diocese of Buffalo. 1966.

Kosnik, James. "Reflections of a Pilgrim Organist: Conversion to Conviction." *Pastoral Music*, Volume 41:5, September 2017.

"Laborers in the Vineyard: Dr. Caspar Koch-Paul Koch-Leo Horvoka." *Cecilia*, Volume 81-82, March-April 1954.

"Lancaster Family Has Six Organists; All Play Weekly in WNY Churches." NP/ND.

Margaret M. (Roy) Rozler Notice, Record for M. Rozler at Ancestry. com.

Miller, C. Eugene. *Gothic Grandeur: A Rare Tradition in American Catholicism.* Buffalo NY: Canisius College Press, 2003.

"Monsignor Paul J. Eberz Dies; Leader in Race Relations, Liturgy." *The Buffalo News*, September 10, 1991.

Most Reverend Edward Michael Grosz, Auxiliary Bishop of Buffalo. Accessed August 16. 2020. https://www.buffalodiocese.org/bishop-grosz.

Muehlbauer, Lisa. "Organists Wear Many Hats But Share Laurel of Devotion." *Buffalo Evening News.* September 8, 1973.

"Sister Mary Grace Ryan, SSMN" *Muzart,* March-April 1972, Volume XXIV, no. 4.

Nease, David. Interview by Bill Fay. May 15, 2017.

Nemmers, Sister M. Helen. "The Catholic Normal School of St. Francis Wisconsin and Its Effect upon Catholic Musical Reform in the United States." MA diss., Catholic University of America, Washington, DC, 1969.

O'Connor, Francis Msgr. *1965 Catholic Directory of the Diocese of Buffalo.* Buffalo NY: The Magnificat, 1965.

"A Preview of Activities at the Thirteenth National Convention." *Muzart,* Volume 12, no. 5, 1960.

Pytak, Alice. "Church Musicians Guild of Buffalo: 50 Years of Ministry 1946-1996." NP/ND.

Rozler, Joseph. Interview by Bill Fay and Michael Riester.

Roy, Eileen. Interview by Bill Fay. June 15, 2018.

Ryan, Sister Mary Grace. "The Progress of Liturgical Music in the United States Since 1903." MM diss., Catholic University of America, 1941.

Ryan, Sister Mary Grace. The Student Notebook *Muzart,* Volume VIII, no.1, 1955.

Ryan, Sister Mary Grace. Papers. Sisters of Saint Mary of Namur archives, Buffalo NY.

The Liturgical Music Award: Society of Saint Gregory. The Catholic Choirmaster. Vol XLV No.III.1959

"Liturgical Medal Won by Woman Musician." NP ND

Stiefermann, Barbarlie. *Stanislaus with Feet in the World: Historical Biography of Mother M. Stanislaus Hegner.* Baltimore MD: Gateway Press, 1990.

"To Our Cecelia: Liturgical Music Award of 1959." Ethel Grabenstter, editor, *Quilisma,* Volume III, no. 5.

Wagner, Myron. "Rev. John B. Singenberger 1848-1924." MA diss., Catholic University of America, 1966.

Wilson Dickson, Andrew. *The Story of Christian Music.* Minneapolis MN: Fortress Press, 1992.

Zadora, Charles. Rev. Paul Eberz. Find a Grave Memorial # 78609632. October 17, 2011.

About the Author

William Fay (Bill) was born in Waterloo, and grew up in Rochester, New York. He attended SUNY Fredonia to study music education. As a college student, Bill got to know Buffalo and moved to the area in 1975. He remembers attending, with his good friend Joanne Jasinski, his first Guild mass in June 1975 at Assumption Church.

Bill taught for 33 years, mostly at LaSalle Senior and Niagara Falls High Schools in Niagara Falls. Near the end of his teaching career, he studied liturgy and church music at the University of Notre Dame for four summers. Taking early retirement, Bill took a position as music director at Saint John XXIII Parish in West Seneca in 2009. He served as director of the Guild from 2013-2019.

Mr. Fay currently serves on the national committee for chapters for the National Association of Pastoral Musicians. His responsibility lies with mentoring chapters in formation.

Made in United States
Orlando, FL
13 May 2022